Devin Nunes: Politics, Power, and Legacy in the Media Age

From Congress to Trump Media: The Controversial Journey of a Conservative Leader

Robert J. Bowers

Copyright © Robert J. Bowers

2024

No part of this book may be reproduced, in any form or by any means, without permission in writing from the publisher, except for the use of brief quotations in a book review.

Table of Contents

Introduction

Chapter 1: Early Life and Education
Background and Family Heritage
Academic Achievements

Chapter 2: Political Career
Early Political Involvement
Tenure in the U.S. House of Representatives

Chapter 3: Key Investigations and Controversies
Role in the Trump-Russia Investigation
The Release of the Controversial Memo on FBI Misconduct

Chapter 4: Transition to Business
Departure from Congress
Role as CEO of Trump Media & Technology Group

Chapter 5: Recent Developments
Appointment as Chairman of the President's Intelligence Advisory Board
Responsibilities and Challenges

Chapter 6: Personal Life
Family and Community Involvement
Philanthropy and Giving Back

Chapter 7: Legacy
Contributions to U.S. Politics and Media
Impact on Public Discourse and Conservative Movements

Conclusion

Introduction

Devin Nunes is a name synonymous with modern conservative politics, media disruption, and the redefinition of intelligence oversight in the United States. Born to a family of farmers in California's Central Valley, Nunes rose from humble beginnings to wield significant influence in the nation's capital. His career, marked by staunch advocacy for his beliefs and bold moves that often courted controversy, has left an indelible mark on the political and media landscape.

From representing California's 21st and 22nd Congressional Districts in the U.S. House of Representatives to chairing the powerful House Intelligence Committee, Nunes has been at the center of pivotal moments in recent American history. Whether leading high-profile investigations or defending his values against fierce criticism, Nunes has consistently portrayed himself as a fighter for transparency and accountability. Now, as Chairman of the President's Intelligence Advisory Board, he stands poised to influence the future of U.S. national security policy.

But Devin Nunes is not merely a politician. His departure from Congress to helm the Trump Media

& Technology Group (TMTG) in 2022 showcased his willingness to embrace new challenges and shift the media narrative for conservative voices. This biography captures the essence of a man driven by conviction, shaped by his upbringing, and determined to leave a legacy of significance. Devin Nunes' political journey has taken an intriguing turn with his recent appointment as Chairman of the President's Intelligence Advisory Board. This role positions him at the intersection of intelligence oversight and policy, with implications that stretch far beyond the boundaries of partisanship.

This new chapter in Nunes' life comes amid a broader conversation about the role of intelligence agencies in protecting democracy while maintaining public trust. His ability to navigate these challenges will likely define the latter part of his career. It also reflects a remarkable shift—from lawmaker to businessman and now to one of the most influential voices in shaping America's intelligence strategy. But what makes Nunes' career so compelling is the emotional undercurrent that runs through his story. As the son of a farming family, his values were shaped by hard work, resilience, and a deep sense of duty to his community.

Those values have guided his actions, even as he faced public scrutiny and political opposition. For his supporters, Nunes embodies the fight for transparency in a time of political turbulence. To his critics, he represents the divisive nature of today's politics. Regardless of perspective, his story is one of unyielding determination and the courage to pursue his vision, regardless of the odds.

Throughout his political career, Nunes has been a lightning rod for controversy. His leadership during the Trump-Russia investigation cemented his reputation as a fearless advocate for what he believes to be the truth. The controversial memo he released in 2018, which alleged FBI misconduct, was both lauded and lambasted, depending on one's political leanings. Yet, for Nunes, the goal was clear: to hold powerful institutions accountable. This willingness to tackle contentious issues head-on has endeared him to many on the right, who see him as a rare politician unafraid to challenge the status quo. However, it has also made him a polarizing figure, with detractors accusing him of partisanship. These conflicting views make Nunes an undeniably fascinating character in American politics.

One of the most remarkable aspects of Devin Nunes' career is his transition from politics to the media world. When he resigned from Congress to become CEO of TMTG, it was seen as a bold move, even for a man known for taking risks. TMTG, the parent company of Truth Social, aimed to provide a platform for conservative voices in an era when traditional social media platforms were accused of censorship. Under Nunes' leadership, the platform became a rallying point for conservatives frustrated with mainstream media and big tech. His role in this media revolution speaks to his adaptability and willingness to embrace new arenas of influence.

What makes Devin Nunes' story resonate beyond political and media circles is its deeply human foundation. Raised in a farming community, he understands the struggles of everyday Americans in a way that few career politicians can. His early life, marked by labor on his family's dairy farm, instilled in him a work ethic and resilience that have defined his career. These roots have also shaped his political philosophy. For Nunes, policies are not abstract concepts but tools to improve the lives of people like his neighbors and family. This connection to his upbringing has made him a relatable figure to many, even as his actions on the national stage spark debate.

His detractors, of course, see him in a different light. To them, Nunes represents the hyper-partisan politics that have fractured American discourse. Yet even his critics would admit that he is a man who acts with conviction, a trait that sets him apart in an era of political calculation and ambiguity. As Devin Nunes steps into his role as Chairman of the President's Intelligence Advisory Board, his story continues to evolve. This new position marks not just a continuation of his career but a potential redefinition of his legacy.

Will he be remembered as a champion of transparency and accountability, or will his critics' narratives overshadow his accomplishments? The answer to that question lies in how he navigates the challenges of his new role, as well as how history ultimately views the turbulent years of his political career. What is undeniable is that Nunes has already left a profound impact on American politics and media. His journey, from the fields of California's Central Valley to the corridors of power in Washington, D.C., and the boardrooms of a media company, is a testament to his ambition and adaptability.

This biography seeks to capture the complexity of Devin Nunes—not just the politician or the media executive, but the man. It delves into his triumphs and controversies, his values and strategies, and his ongoing quest to shape the future of America.

In telling his story, we uncover not just the details of his career but the emotional and moral underpinnings of a life dedicated to making a difference. Whether loved or criticized, Devin Nunes remains a figure who cannot be ignored. His legacy, as it continues to unfold, will be one of resilience, determination, and the unyielding pursuit of his vision.

Chapter 1: Early Life and Education

Background and Family Heritage

Devin Gerald Nunes was born on October 1, 1973, in Tulare, California, a small agricultural town nestled in the heart of the San Joaquin Valley. His family roots run deep in the region, with a heritage that reflects the perseverance and industriousness of farming communities. His grandparents immigrated to the United States from Portugal's Azores Islands in the early 20th century, seeking better opportunities. Like many immigrant families, the Nuneses brought with them a strong work ethic, a sense of community, and an unwavering commitment to family values.

The Nunes family operated a dairy farm in Tulare County, a demanding profession that shaped Devin's character from a young age. Growing up, he worked alongside his father and brother, developing a firsthand understanding of the challenges faced by farmers. The cyclical nature of agriculture—dependent on weather, market prices, and policy decisions—taught him the importance of resilience and adaptability.

For Devin, these early experiences were formative. They instilled in him a profound respect for hard work and a deep connection to the land and the people who worked it. This connection would later influence his political philosophy, driving his advocacy for rural communities and agricultural policies during his time in Congress.

Academic Achievements

Despite the long hours spent working on the farm, education was a priority in the Nunes household. Devin attended public schools in Tulare County, where he excelled academically. His natural curiosity and determination were evident from an early age, traits that his teachers and peers often noted. After graduating from Tulare Union High School, Nunes pursued higher education at College of the Sequoias, a community college in Visalia, California. This decision reflected his pragmatic approach to life; attending a local institution allowed him to remain close to home while saving money. At College of the Sequoias, he earned an associate's degree before transferring to California Polytechnic State University (Cal Poly) in San Luis Obispo.

At Cal Poly, Nunes majored in agricultural business, a field that aligned with his upbringing and future aspirations. He demonstrated a keen interest in understanding the broader economic and policy issues affecting agriculture. His professors recall him as a diligent student who asked probing questions and showed a genuine interest in finding solutions to the challenges faced by farmers and rural communities.

Nunes' academic achievements extended beyond the classroom. He earned a master's degree in agriculture from Cal Poly, further solidifying his expertise in the field. His advanced studies equipped him with a comprehensive understanding of agricultural markets, supply chains, and policy frameworks—knowledge that would later prove invaluable in his political career. While Nunes' academic pursuits were deeply tied to his roots, he was also beginning to see a larger picture. As he delved into the complexities of agricultural economics and policy, he became increasingly aware of the disconnect between policymakers and the communities they served. This realization planted the seeds of a political career focused on bridging that gap.

Nunes' time at Cal Poly was marked by a growing interest in public service. He closely followed local and national politics, paying particular attention to issues affecting the agricultural sector. His passion for advocating on behalf of farmers and rural communities was evident to those who knew him. Friends and mentors often remarked on his ability to articulate complex issues in a way that was both relatable and persuasive—a skill that would serve him well in the years to come.

In addition to his academic and professional ambitions, Nunes was deeply influenced by his family's values. His parents, Antonio and Toni Diane, emphasized the importance of community involvement and standing up for what is right. These lessons would shape his approach to leadership and his commitment to representing his constituents. Devin Nunes' early life is a story of contrasts: the rugged, hands-on work of a dairy farm juxtaposed with the analytical rigor of academic study. This dual perspective gave him a unique ability to understand both the practical challenges faced by farmers and the systemic issues that shaped agricultural policy. For Nunes, these two worlds were not separate but interconnected.

He saw politics as a way to address the structural problems that often left rural communities feeling overlooked and underserved. His background gave him credibility among his peers in the farming community, while his education equipped him to navigate the complexities of public policy. This combination of lived experience and academic expertise set Nunes apart from many of his contemporaries. It also positioned him as a natural leader, someone who could bridge the divide between local concerns and national decision-making.

As a young man, Devin Nunes was already formulating a vision for the future—one rooted in the belief that rural communities deserved a stronger voice in government. He saw firsthand how policies made in Washington, D.C., could have profound effects on the lives of farmers and their families. Whether it was water rights, trade agreements, or environmental regulations, Nunes understood that these issues were not abstract but deeply personal. This vision would later become the foundation of his political career. His goal was not just to represent his constituents but to advocate for a way of life that he believed was essential to America's identity.

For Nunes, agriculture was not just an industry; it was a cornerstone of the nation's economy, culture, and values. At the same time, Nunes was acutely aware of the challenges facing rural America. The rise of urbanization, changing economic dynamics, and shifting political priorities often left agricultural communities at a disadvantage. These challenges fueled his determination to make a difference, to ensure that the voices of people like his family and neighbors were heard in the halls of power.

Devin Nunes' early life and education were defined by a sense of purpose and possibility. From the fields of Tulare County to the classrooms of Cal Poly, he cultivated the skills, knowledge, and values that would shape his future. As he prepared to enter the world of politics, Nunes carried with him the lessons of his upbringing: the importance of hard work, the value of community, and the conviction to stand up for what he believed in. These principles would guide him as he embarked on a career that would take him from California's Central Valley to the forefront of national and international debates. In many ways, the story of Devin Nunes' early life is a testament to the power of determination and the enduring influence of one's roots.

It is a story that speaks to the challenges and opportunities of bridging two worlds—farming and politics—and the transformative potential of a clear vision and unwavering commitment. As we move forward in this biography, we will see how these formative years laid the groundwork for a career marked by ambition, controversy, and impact. From his first forays into politics to his rise as a national figure, Devin Nunes' journey is one of resilience, adaptability, and the relentless pursuit of his goals.

Chapter 2: Political Career

Early Political Involvement

Devin Nunes' political journey began not with the glamour of national campaigns but with a deep commitment to his community and an innate understanding of its challenges. Fresh out of college, armed with degrees in agricultural business and a passion for advocacy, Nunes decided to take his first steps into public service.

In 1996, at just 23 years old, he made a bold move by running for the Tulare County Board of Education. While many viewed his youth as a disadvantage, Nunes turned it into an asset, demonstrating energy and fresh ideas. His election to the board marked the beginning of a career centered on public service. During his tenure, Nunes worked to improve educational opportunities in the rural district, particularly emphasizing programs that would benefit children from agricultural communities like his own. This early experience provided him with a valuable understanding of governance and policy making. It also gave him a taste of what it meant to represent the needs of others, a lesson that would prove invaluable as his career advanced.

Tenure in the U.S. House of Representatives

In 2002, Devin Nunes launched a campaign for Congress, seeking to represent California's 21st district. His platform was a reflection of his roots: advocating for agriculture, rural development, and water access in the drought-prone Central Valley. Nunes' message resonated with voters, and at the age of 29, he became one of the youngest members of Congress.

Over time, Nunes' district would change through redistricting, becoming California's 22nd district, but his priorities remained consistent. He quickly established himself as a staunch advocate for farmers, frequently emphasizing the importance of water rights in the arid Central Valley. To Nunes, the region's ability to thrive depended on reliable access to water, a resource often mired in contentious political and environmental debates. Nunes also championed conservative economic policies, including tax reform and reducing government overreach. He became a reliable ally to Republican leadership, earning a reputation as a disciplined and focused legislator.

His ability to navigate the complexities of Washington, while maintaining a connection to his constituents, set him apart from many of his peers. In 2015, Nunes was appointed chairman of the House Permanent Select Committee on Intelligence, one of the most prestigious and sensitive roles in Congress. This position placed him at the center of key national security debates and afforded him significant influence over U.S. intelligence policies.

As chairman, Nunes prioritized oversight of intelligence agencies, focusing on issues like cybersecurity threats, counterterrorism, and foreign influence. However, his tenure was defined by his involvement in high-profile investigations, which thrust him into the national spotlight. Nunes' chairmanship coincided with one of the most politically charged periods in recent history: the investigation into Russian interference in the 2016 presidential election. The House Intelligence Committee played a critical role in this inquiry, and Nunes found himself at the center of a contentious and deeply partisan battle. Initially, the committee sought to conduct a bipartisan investigation into Russian meddling and potential collusion with the Trump campaign.

However, tensions quickly escalated as Nunes faced accusations of bias due to his close ties to the Trump administration. Critics argued that his actions, including his decision to brief President Trump on classified information without consulting his Democratic counterparts, compromised the investigation's credibility. Supporters, on the other hand, praised Nunes for his loyalty and determination to expose what he viewed as misconduct within federal agencies. His staunch defense of Trump made him a hero among conservative circles, while simultaneously earning the ire of Democrats and some moderates.

One of the most defining moments of Nunes' career was the release of a four-page memo in February 2018. The memo, authored by Nunes and his staff, alleged misconduct by the FBI and the Department of Justice during their investigation into the Trump campaign's ties to Russia. Specifically, it claimed that the FBI had improperly used a dossier funded by Democratic sources to obtain surveillance warrants against Trump campaign adviser Carter Page. The memo's release sparked a firestorm of controversy. Republicans hailed it as proof of systemic bias within federal agencies, while Democrats dismissed it as a politically motivated distraction.

The episode cemented Nunes' reputation as one of Trump's most ardent defenders and underscored his willingness to take on the intelligence establishment. For Nunes, the memo represented more than just a political maneuver. It reflected his broader concerns about government transparency and accountability. Whether one viewed him as a whistleblower or a partisan operative, there was no denying the impact of his actions on the national discourse.

While the Russia investigation dominated headlines, Nunes never abandoned the issues closest to his heart: agriculture and water policy. Throughout his tenure, he remained a vocal advocate for the Central Valley, frequently pushing for legislation to address the region's chronic water shortages. Nunes worked to secure federal funding for water infrastructure projects, including the construction and maintenance of reservoirs and canals. He also fought against regulations that he believed unfairly limited water access for farmers, arguing that environmental policies often prioritized wildlife over human needs. For his constituents, these efforts were a reminder that Nunes had not lost sight of the people who first sent him to Congress.

His ability to balance local concerns with national responsibilities was a hallmark of his career, even as his role on the Intelligence Committee garnered more attention. Devin Nunes' political career has been marked by both praise and criticism, often in equal measure. Supporters laud him as a principled leader who is unafraid to challenge the status quo, while detractors accuse him of partisanship and self-serving behavior.

One of the most significant criticisms came during the height of the Russia investigation, when Nunes faced calls to recuse himself from the inquiry due to allegations of conflicts of interest. Despite the backlash, he refused to step aside, arguing that his actions were in the best interest of transparency and accountability. Throughout these controversies, Nunes maintained a steadfast commitment to his beliefs. Whether one agrees with his positions or not, his resolve has been a defining characteristic of his career. Devin Nunes served in the U.S. House of Representatives for nearly two decades, leaving a lasting imprint on both his district and the national stage. His advocacy for rural communities, particularly in the realms of water policy and agriculture, remains a cornerstone of his legacy.

At the same time, his tenure on the Intelligence Committee marked a turning point in his career, transforming him from a relatively low-profile congressman into a polarizing figure in American politics. For better or worse, Nunes became a symbol of the deeply partisan divide that has come to define Washington in recent years.

In 2021, Nunes announced his decision to leave Congress, a move that surprised many and signaled the beginning of a new chapter in his career. As he transitioned from legislator to business leader, the impact of his time in Congress continued to resonate, both in his home district and across the nation. Devin Nunes' political career was anything but conventional. It was a journey defined by ambition, controversy, and an unwavering commitment to his principles. As we move into the next chapter, we will explore his decision to leave politics and embark on a new path, one that reflects both his loyalty to former President Trump and his desire to shape the future of media and technology.

Chapter 3: Key Investigations and Controversies

Role in the Trump-Russia Investigation

Devin Nunes' tenure as Chairman of the House Intelligence Committee coincided with one of the most contentious and politically charged investigations in modern U.S. history: the probe into Russian interference in the 2016 presidential election. For Nunes, this investigation became a defining chapter in his career, showcasing his loyalty to President Donald Trump while igniting fierce debates about partisanship and the role of congressional oversight.

The investigation's origins lay in the intelligence community's conclusion that Russia had interfered in the 2016 election to bolster Trump's chances of winning. This assertion led to multiple inquiries, including one by Special Counsel Robert Mueller and another by the House Intelligence Committee. Nunes, as chairman, oversaw the committee's efforts, making him a central figure in the unfolding drama.

Initially, the committee's investigation aimed to examine the scope of Russian interference and potential ties to Trump's campaign. However, it quickly became a political battleground. Nunes, a close ally of Trump, faced accusations of using his position to shield the president from scrutiny. Democrats on the committee argued that Nunes was more focused on discrediting the investigation than uncovering the truth.

One of the most controversial moments came in March 2017, when Nunes made an unexpected public statement claiming he had seen classified evidence suggesting that members of Trump's transition team had been improperly surveilled by U.S. intelligence agencies. The statement caused an uproar, with critics accusing Nunes of attempting to distract from the investigation into Russia's election interference. Nunes defended his actions, arguing that his revelations were in the public interest and exposed potential abuses of power within the intelligence community. This incident led to calls for Nunes to recuse himself from the investigation. While Nunes temporarily stepped aside from leading the inquiry, he remained deeply involved, and his influence on the process was undeniable.

The Release of the Controversial Memo on FBI Misconduct

The controversy surrounding Nunes reached its peak in early 2018 with the release of a four-page memo that he and his staff had drafted. Known simply as "the Nunes memo," it alleged serious misconduct by the FBI and the Department of Justice during their investigation into Trump's campaign. Specifically, the memo accused the FBI of using unverified information from the Steele dossier—a document funded in part by Democratic sources—to obtain a Foreign Intelligence Surveillance Act (FISA) warrant against Carter Page, a former Trump campaign adviser.

For Nunes and his allies, the memo was a bombshell. They argued that it exposed a pattern of bias and misconduct within federal law enforcement agencies, undermining the legitimacy of the Russia investigation. Republicans hailed the memo as proof of a "deep state" conspiracy to undermine Trump's presidency. The process leading up to the memo's release was fraught with controversy. Nunes faced accusations of cherry-picking information and presenting a one-sided narrative.

The FBI and DOJ publicly objected to the release, warning that it omitted critical context and could compromise national security. Despite these objections, the memo was declassified and released to the public in February 2018, sparking a political firestorm. Democrats on the committee, led by ranking member Adam Schiff, responded with their own memo, which sought to counter Nunes' claims and provide additional context. They argued that the FISA warrant against Page was justified and that the Steele dossier was only a small part of the evidence used to obtain it. Schiff accused Nunes of using his position to carry out a partisan attack on the FBI and DOJ in an effort to protect Trump.

The release of the Nunes memo had far-reaching consequences. It deepened the partisan divide over the Russia investigation and further eroded public trust in federal institutions. For his supporters, Nunes emerged as a courageous whistleblower willing to challenge the intelligence establishment. For his detractors, he became a symbol of partisan overreach and a key player in the effort to undermine an investigation of national importance. The fallout from the Nunes memo highlighted the growing polarization in American politics.

For conservatives, the memo validated their long-standing concerns about bias within the FBI and DOJ. Fox News and other right-leaning outlets praised Nunes for exposing what they saw as systemic corruption, while Trump himself tweeted that the memo "totally vindicates" him in the Russia investigation.

On the other hand, critics argued that the memo was a calculated attempt to discredit the investigation and shift attention away from Trump's potential wrongdoing. Legal experts questioned the accuracy of Nunes' claims, noting that much of the information used to obtain the FISA warrant against Carter Page remained classified and could not be independently verified. The controversy also had broader implications for congressional oversight. Nunes' actions raised questions about the role of partisanship in oversight committees, which are traditionally expected to operate in a bipartisan manner. The feud between Nunes and Schiff, in particular, underscored the challenges of conducting meaningful oversight in an era of extreme political polarization. For Devin Nunes, the release of the memo and his broader involvement in the Russia investigation were about more than defending Trump.

In his view, the controversies surrounding the investigation exposed fundamental problems within the intelligence community, including a lack of transparency and accountability. Nunes argued that the public had a right to know how surveillance tools were being used and whether they were being misused for political purposes.

In interviews and public statements, Nunes framed himself as a truth-seeker, someone willing to take on powerful institutions in defense of the Constitution. He rejected accusations of partisanship, insisting that his actions were motivated by a commitment to justice and fairness. However, critics pointed to Nunes' close relationship with Trump as evidence of bias. They argued that his actions were less about uncovering the truth and more about protecting the president from scrutiny. Nunes' decision to brief Trump on classified information without consulting his committee colleagues further fueled these accusations, with many questioning whether he had compromised the integrity of the investigation. Devin Nunes' role in the Trump-Russia investigation cemented his status as one of the most polarizing figures in American politics.

To his supporters, he was a hero, a fearless defender of conservative values and a champion of government accountability. To his detractors, he was a partisan operative who undermined the credibility of a critical investigation and damaged public trust in federal institutions. The controversies surrounding Nunes' actions reflected the broader political climate of the time, marked by deep divisions and an erosion of bipartisan cooperation. His willingness to take bold, controversial steps made him a lightning rod for criticism but also earned him a devoted following among Trump supporters.

The Nunes memo remains a defining moment in Devin Nunes' career, encapsulating both his strengths and his vulnerabilities as a political leader. It demonstrated his ability to command attention and shape the national narrative, but it also highlighted the risks of partisanship in highly sensitive investigations. For better or worse, the memo's release had a lasting impact on the Russia investigation, public perceptions of the FBI and DOJ, and Nunes' own political legacy. It solidified his reputation as a loyal Trump ally and a controversial figure willing to challenge the status quo.

As Nunes transitioned from Congress to the private sector, the legacy of his involvement in the Russia investigation continued to follow him. While his supporters viewed him as a principled advocate for transparency, his critics saw him as a cautionary tale about the dangers of politicizing oversight.

In the next chapter, we will explore Nunes' decision to leave Congress and his new role as CEO of Trump Media & Technology Group, a move that reflected both his loyalty to Trump and his desire to influence the future of media and technology.

Chapter 4: Transition to Business

Departure from Congress

Devin Nunes' decision to leave Congress in 2022 shocked political observers and signaled a major shift in his career trajectory. After serving nearly two decades in the U.S. House of Representatives, Nunes announced he would not seek reelection, opting instead to become CEO of Trump Media & Technology Group (TMTG), the company behind the social media platform Truth Social.

The move surprised even some of Nunes' staunchest allies. As a senior member of Congress with considerable influence, he had long been a fixture in the Republican Party. Leaving behind a promising future in politics to join the business world was unconventional for someone with his stature, but for Nunes, it was a calculated decision. His departure reflected the deep bond he had forged with Donald Trump during his time in Congress. Nunes had consistently aligned himself with the former president's agenda and had become one of Trump's most vocal defenders.

The opportunity to lead TMTG gave Nunes a new platform to champion conservative values and push back against what he saw as censorship by Big Tech companies. In his resignation announcement, Nunes framed the transition as a natural extension of his mission to protect free speech and challenge the dominance of Silicon Valley. "The time has come to reopen the Internet and allow for the free flow of ideas and expression without fear of being silenced," he stated. His words struck a chord with conservatives who felt alienated by mainstream social media platforms like Twitter and Facebook.

Role as CEO of Trump Media & Technology Group

Taking the reins as CEO of TMTG was no small task. The company had ambitious goals: to create a social media platform that could rival established giants and provide a safe space for conservative voices. For Nunes, the position was both an opportunity and a challenge. Nunes entered the role with little prior experience in the tech industry, but his political background and loyalty to Trump made him a natural fit for the job. As CEO, he was responsible for overseeing the development and growth of Truth Social, a platform designed to counter what many conservatives perceived as liberal bias in mainstream media.

The launch of Truth Social in early 2022 was met with both excitement and skepticism. Supporters hailed it as a long-overdue alternative to platforms like Twitter, which had banned Trump following the January 6th Capitol riot. Critics, however, questioned whether the platform could achieve its lofty goals or attract a broad enough user base to sustain itself.

Under Nunes' leadership, TMTG faced significant hurdles. Technical glitches and delays marred the initial rollout of Truth Social, leading to frustration among users and negative press coverage. Despite these challenges, Nunes remained optimistic, emphasizing the platform's potential to reshape the media landscape. He frequently highlighted Truth Social's commitment to free speech and its promise to give everyday Americans a voice. Nunes' transition from politics to business was driven by a broader mission: to challenge the power and influence of Big Tech companies. Throughout his political career, he had been a vocal critic of Silicon Valley, accusing platforms like Twitter, Facebook, and YouTube of suppressing conservative viewpoints.

As CEO of TMTG, Nunes saw an opportunity to build a company that could compete with these tech giants and provide an alternative for conservatives who felt marginalized. He framed the fight against Big Tech as a battle for free speech and democratic values, positioning TMTG as a beacon of hope for those disillusioned with traditional social media platforms.

However, the road was far from easy. Competing with established companies required significant resources, technical expertise, and user engagement. While Truth Social quickly gained traction among Trump supporters, critics argued that its limited appeal and niche audience would hinder its long-term success. Despite these challenges, Nunes remained steadfast in his mission. He frequently spoke about the importance of diversifying the media landscape and giving Americans more choices in how they consume information. His leadership at TMTG reflected his deep belief in the power of technology to shape public discourse and empower individuals. Even after leaving Congress, Nunes continued to play a prominent role in conservative politics.

His position at TMTG allowed him to remain closely connected to Trump and the broader Republican movement, ensuring that his voice remained influential in national debates. Nunes used his platform to advocate for conservative values and push back against perceived liberal bias in the media. He frequently criticized mainstream news outlets and social media platforms, accusing them of spreading misinformation and suppressing dissenting opinions.

At the same time, Nunes faced scrutiny for his close ties to Trump and his role in promoting Truth Social. Critics argued that his involvement with the platform blurred the lines between business and politics, raising questions about the ethical implications of his new position. Some also pointed to the financial challenges facing TMTG, questioning whether the company could achieve its ambitious goals in a competitive and rapidly evolving tech landscape. Nunes' transition to business marked a significant shift in his career, but it also underscored his enduring commitment to the causes he championed in Congress. His decision to leave politics reflected a willingness to take risks and embrace new challenges, even in the face of uncertainty.

For Nunes, leading TMTG was not just about building a successful company; it was about shaping the future of media and technology in a way that aligned with his values. He saw Truth Social as more than a business venture—it was a platform for change, a tool for amplifying voices that he believed had been silenced for too long. While the long-term success of TMTG remains uncertain, Nunes' leadership has already left a mark on the conservative movement. His willingness to step away from a secure political career to pursue a bold new vision speaks to his determination and resilience.

Public reaction to Nunes' role at TMTG has been polarized, much like his political career. Supporters praise him for taking on Big Tech and providing a voice for conservatives in the digital space. They view his leadership at TMTG as a continuation of his fight for free speech and government accountability. Critics, however, remain skeptical of his motives and question the viability of Truth Social. Some have accused Nunes of using his position at TMTG to further Trump's political agenda, rather than focusing on building a sustainable business.

Others have pointed to the challenges facing the platform, including technical issues, financial constraints, and a limited user base. Despite these criticisms, Nunes has remained undeterred. He frequently emphasizes the importance of resilience and innovation, drawing parallels between his experiences in politics and his new role in business. For Nunes, the challenges facing TMTG are opportunities to prove his critics wrong and demonstrate the power of conservative entrepreneurship.

As Devin Nunes continues to navigate his new role as CEO of TMTG, the future remains uncertain but full of potential. His journey from Congress to the business world reflects a willingness to adapt and evolve, embracing new opportunities while staying true to his core values. In the next chapter, we will explore Nunes' recent appointment as Chairman of the President's Intelligence Advisory Board, a role that further cements his influence in national security and underscores his enduring commitment to public service. This development marks yet another chapter in a career defined by bold decisions, unwavering principles, and a relentless pursuit of change.

Chapter 5: Recent Developments

Appointment as Chairman of the President's Intelligence Advisory Board

Devin Nunes' appointment as Chairman of the President's Intelligence Advisory Board (PIAB) marked a pivotal moment in his career, signaling his enduring influence in national security and governance. Announced in late 2024, this prestigious role reaffirmed Nunes' standing as a key figure in shaping America's intelligence policies, even after leaving Congress.

The PIAB, established during the Eisenhower administration, serves as a direct advisory body to the President on matters of national intelligence. Its members are chosen for their expertise and dedication to safeguarding national security. As chairman, Nunes assumed a critical position, tasked with reviewing the performance of the intelligence community and providing independent assessments of its operations. This role not only elevated Nunes' profile but also demonstrated the trust placed in him by key figures in Washington.

For a man whose career has often been defined by controversy and staunch conservatism, the appointment symbolized a shift in perception: from partisan political player to a statesman entrusted with one of the nation's most sensitive responsibilities.

Responsibilities and Challenges

As chairman of the PIAB, Nunes faced an array of complex challenges. His primary responsibilities included evaluating the efficiency and effectiveness of U.S. intelligence agencies, identifying potential gaps or vulnerabilities, and ensuring that the President received accurate and timely information to make informed decisions.BOne of the key issues on his agenda was addressing the growing threat of cyber warfare. In a rapidly evolving digital landscape, foreign adversaries such as China, Russia, and Iran were increasingly leveraging cyberattacks to disrupt American infrastructure and steal sensitive information. Nunes, who had long advocated for stronger cybersecurity measures, was well-suited to tackle this pressing issue. Under his leadership, the board began an in-depth review of the nation's cybersecurity defenses, emphasizing the need for greater coordination between government agencies and private sector partners.

Nunes' experience in Congress, where he had championed legislation to modernize the intelligence community, proved invaluable in crafting strategies to enhance the country's resilience against cyber threats. Another critical focus was the challenge of balancing civil liberties with national security. The post-9/11 era had seen significant expansions in surveillance capabilities, raising concerns about privacy and government overreach. As chairman, Nunes was tasked with ensuring that intelligence operations remained both effective and constitutionally sound. This delicate balancing act required a nuanced understanding of legal and ethical considerations, as well as a commitment to transparency and accountability.

Nunes' appointment carried significant political and strategic implications. For one, it reinforced his status as a trusted ally of conservative leadership and a key player in shaping the nation's intelligence priorities. His tenure as chairman was expected to influence not only the direction of U.S. intelligence policy but also the broader discourse surrounding national security. Critics, however, raised questions about Nunes' suitability for the role.

Some argued that his deeply partisan approach during his time in Congress, particularly his handling of the Trump-Russia investigation, made him a controversial choice for a position that demanded impartiality. Others pointed to his close ties to Donald Trump, suggesting that his appointment was as much a political reward as a recognition of his qualifications.

Despite these criticisms, Nunes approached his new role with characteristic determination. In public statements, he emphasized his commitment to ensuring the integrity of the intelligence community and safeguarding the nation against emerging threats. "This is not about politics,"

Chapter 6: Personal Life

Devin Nunes, the political figure who has navigated the tumultuous waters of American governance, has always kept his personal life relatively private. Unlike many public figures, Nunes has managed to retain an air of mystery around his family and personal interests, focusing primarily on his public career. However, his life outside of politics plays a crucial role in understanding the man behind the political persona.

Family and Community Involvement

Nunes was born and raised in Tulare, California, a small town in the heart of the San Joaquin Valley. The influence of his family and his upbringing in rural California shaped much of his worldview and values. He grew up in a farming community, where hard work and family traditions were paramount. His father, a dairy farmer, and his mother, who worked as a teacher, instilled in him a deep appreciation for the land and the importance of community. Throughout his political career, Nunes has often referenced his agricultural background.

It is clear that his roots in farming have played a significant role in his political identity, especially when it comes to advocating for policies that benefit rural communities. In particular, he has been a staunch advocate for the interests of farmers and agricultural workers, pushing for government policies that support the industry and protect the livelihoods of families like his own. His work on the House Agriculture Committee was an extension of these values, allowing him to serve as a champion for those who he believes are often overlooked in Washington's power corridors.

While Nunes' political career may have taken him to Washington, he has remained grounded in his roots. He is known for his deep connection to his hometown of Tulare, where he continues to be involved in local community activities. Nunes regularly returns to his district in California to meet with constituents and participate in events that strengthen his bond with the community. His commitment to his local roots has earned him respect among the people who knew him before he became a national figure. Despite his rise to political prominence, he has maintained a sense of loyalty to the people and place that shaped him.

Family is at the core of Nunes' personal life. He is married to Elizabeth Nunes, and together they have three children. Elizabeth, a former teacher, has been an integral part of Devin's life, and their partnership has been central to his success in both his personal and professional spheres. They are a family that values privacy, which is why Nunes' personal life has largely remained out of the public eye. However, his devotion to his wife and children is evident in the way he speaks about them in interviews and public appearances.

Throughout his career, Nunes has often emphasized the importance of family values and the influence his parents had on his life. He credits much of his drive and work ethic to the lessons he learned from his upbringing. In a 2018 interview, Nunes said, "My parents taught me the value of hard work, integrity, and doing what's right, even when it's not easy. These are the values I've tried to live by throughout my life, both in politics and at home." Though Nunes is best known for his career in politics, he has a number of personal interests and hobbies that provide insight into his personality and passions. A longtime fan of sports, Nunes has been particularly interested in baseball.

Growing up in a small town, he often participated in local sports leagues, and the game of baseball has remained a part of his life. He's known to attend games with his family whenever possible, finding joy in the simplicity of the sport and the camaraderie that it fosters. This connection to baseball highlights Nunes' appreciation for community and shared experiences, values that have influenced his political approach as well.

In addition to sports, Nunes has a deep interest in the outdoors. His love for nature and the environment can be traced back to his childhood in the agricultural heartland of California. Even as a busy congressman and political figure, Nunes has managed to make time for outdoor activities like hiking and fishing. These hobbies, which connect him to the land and his rural roots, provide a balance to his high-pressure career in politics. Nunes is also an avid reader, with a particular interest in history and American politics. His reading habits reflect his deep curiosity about the world and his commitment to understanding the complexities of governance and leadership. Books by political philosophers and works on American history have influenced his views on government, liberty, and the role of the state.

This intellectual pursuit has shaped his approach to policy-making, making him a thinker as much as a doer.

Philanthropy and Giving Back

While Nunes may not be as publicly philanthropic as some other political figures, he has quietly contributed to several charitable causes throughout his life. His family's agricultural background has inspired his commitment to supporting local community initiatives, particularly those that focus on education, healthcare, and rural development.

Nunes has often donated to local charities in Tulare County, providing resources to schools, hospitals, and community organizations. In particular, his contributions to agricultural scholarships and vocational training programs have made a lasting impact on the youth in his community. By investing in the next generation, Nunes has sought to give back to the place that gave him his start. Beyond his immediate community, Nunes has been involved in several national charitable causes, particularly those related to veterans' affairs and military families.

As a politician who has spent much of his career advocating for strong national defense policies, he has used his platform to raise awareness about the challenges faced by veterans and their families. Whether through supporting veterans' charities or speaking at events honoring military service, Nunes has shown a deep respect for the sacrifices made by those who serve the country.

One of the most challenging aspects of Nunes' career has been balancing his public persona with his private life. Like many public figures, he has had to navigate the constant scrutiny that comes with holding office and making controversial decisions. Despite the media attention, Nunes has made a concerted effort to protect his family from the public spotlight. His decision to keep his personal life private is, in part, a reflection of his desire to maintain a sense of normalcy for his children, away from the chaos and conflict of the political world. Yet, his family life has not been entirely shielded from public view. As a prominent Republican figure, Nunes has been the subject of both praise and criticism, which has inevitably affected his loved ones. He has been open in interviews about the emotional toll that political life can take on his family, especially during moments of intense public scrutiny.

In one interview, Nunes remarked, "Politics is tough, but it's even tougher on your family. They don't ask for this life, and they don't deserve the criticism that comes with it." Despite these challenges, Nunes has always spoken with pride about his family's role in his life. Their unwavering support has been one of his greatest sources of strength throughout his career. For Nunes, family is not just an anchor; it is the foundation upon which he has built his life and his legacy. As he continues to navigate the political landscape, it is clear that his commitment to his family and community will remain a guiding force in his future endeavors.

In sum, Nunes' personal life, though somewhat private, reveals a man deeply connected to his roots, values, and family. His commitment to the community, his passion for the outdoors, and his dedication to giving back paint a picture of a man who, despite his political ambitions, has remained grounded in the principles that shaped him. As Nunes continues to evolve in his professional life, it is evident that his personal life will remain the bedrock upon which his career stands.

Chapter 7: Legacy

Devin Nunes' legacy is one that intertwines his contributions to U.S. politics and media with his deep impact on conservative movements and public discourse. Whether one sees him as a staunch advocate of conservative values or as a controversial figure whose decisions and actions sparked heated debate, it is undeniable that Nunes' career has left an indelible mark on both the political landscape and the media ecosystem. As Nunes moves into new chapters of his life—transitioning into media and business—the legacy of his tenure in Congress, his controversial moments, and his influence on conservative ideologies remain potent and relevant.

Contributions to U.S. Politics and Media

Devin Nunes' political journey has been one marked by both significant accomplishments and controversial episodes, with his contributions shaping the landscape of U.S. politics in ways both praised and criticized. Rising from his roots as a farmer's son in California's Central Valley, Nunes served nearly two decades in the U.S. House of Representatives, representing California's 21st and 22nd districts.

Throughout his time in office, he built a reputation as a fiercely loyal advocate for the agricultural sector, a key player in conservative politics, and an unyielding defender of President Donald Trump. Perhaps Nunes' most significant contribution to U.S. politics was his role as Chairman of the House Intelligence Committee. In this position, Nunes became the focal point of the Trump-Russia investigation, leading efforts to investigate allegations of interference in the 2016 U.S. presidential election.

His release of the now-infamous memo in 2018, which accused the FBI of misconduct during the investigation, galvanized both supporters and critics. For his allies, Nunes was a courageous defender of transparency, exposing what they believed was overreach by the FBI and a partisan attack on President Trump. For his critics, Nunes' memo represented a dangerously misleading effort to undermine the integrity of a legitimate investigation. Despite the polarizing nature of his work on the Intelligence Committee, Nunes was undeniably a key player in the ongoing drama of the Trump administration.

As Chairman, he used his position to cast doubt on the investigations into Russian interference, pushing a narrative that aligned closely with Trump's desire to discredit the FBI and the broader intelligence community. His efforts were seen by many as an extension of Trump's own strategy to discredit the investigative process and redirect attention away from any potential misconduct.

Beyond his work on the Intelligence Committee, Nunes' political career also included significant involvement in shaping U.S. policy on issues like agriculture, taxes, and national security. As a member of the House Ways and Means Committee, he worked on several pieces of legislation that aimed to reform the tax system and provide support to rural communities. His advocacy for farmers, often linked to his background in agriculture, made him a prominent voice on issues affecting rural America. Nunes worked tirelessly to pass policies that protected farmers from what he saw as overbearing government regulations and unnecessary taxation. These contributions earned him respect among his constituents in California and among fellow Republicans in Washington, even as his critics contended that his policies disproportionately benefited the wealthy and large corporations.

When Nunes departed Congress to take on a new role as the CEO of Trump Media & Technology Group, he took with him a wealth of experience in shaping policy and public opinion. His transition from politics to media was a natural progression for a man who had become increasingly influential in the conservative movement and media ecosystem.

Under his leadership, the Trump Media & Technology Group made a clear pivot toward creating a media outlet designed to challenge mainstream narratives and provide an alternative voice for conservative Americans. The company's flagship project, Truth Social, a social media platform launched by former President Trump, was seen as an effort to provide a space where conservative viewpoints could thrive without the censorship and scrutiny they believed were imposed by mainstream platforms like Twitter and Facebook. Nunes' work in media is reshaping his legacy, as he becomes a key figure in the effort to create media outlets that cater to a conservative audience. His leadership at Trump Media & Technology Group places him squarely in the midst of the ongoing battle over the role of media in modern political discourse.

For many, Nunes' pivot to media represents the next logical step in his career—a man who has spent years shaping public opinion now using his platform to build a media empire designed to amplify conservative voices. Critics, however, see this transition as one more example of his embrace of controversial, partisan approaches to both politics and media, seeing him as a figure who continues to promote narratives that they believe undermine objective truth and the integrity of the political process.

Impact on Public Discourse and Conservative Movements

Devin Nunes' role in shaping public discourse, particularly in the context of conservative movements, cannot be overstated. Over the course of his career, he became a prominent figure in the Republican Party and was widely regarded as a defender of conservative values. His work in Congress, particularly his defense of President Trump, marked him as a central figure in the rise of what many have termed the "Trumpist" movement—an ideological shift within the Republican Party toward nationalism, populism, and a fierce resistance to the political establishment.

Nunes' commitment to Trump's agenda placed him at the heart of one of the most contentious periods in modern American politics. His unwavering support for Trump, even during the most turbulent moments of the Trump administration, earned him both fervent supporters and fierce critics. For his supporters, Nunes was a hero—a politician willing to stand up to the so-called "deep state" and fight back against a political system they believed was rigged against ordinary Americans. His strong stance on issues like immigration, taxation, and government regulation resonated deeply with conservatives who felt left behind by traditional political elites.

For Nunes' detractors, however, his embrace of Trumpism and his role in championing Trump's policies contributed to the fragmentation of American politics. His involvement in the Trump-Russia investigation, particularly the memo he released accusing the FBI of bias, symbolized what many saw as a broader effort to undermine American institutions and erode public trust in the democratic process. The release of the memo, in particular, led to accusations that Nunes was sacrificing truth and integrity for political gain—a charge that has followed him throughout his career.

Moreover, Nunes' pivot to media with Trump Media & Technology Group has been viewed as a natural extension of his ideological commitment to conservative values. His transition into media leadership has amplified his influence in the conservative sphere, where he now plays a significant role in shaping the narratives that guide conservative thought. By promoting media platforms like Truth Social, Nunes has embraced the role of media mogul, using his platform to challenge what he and his supporters perceive as liberal bias in mainstream media.

Through this lens, his work in media is not just about providing an alternative to traditional outlets; it's about challenging the very foundation of how information is disseminated in America. Nunes' influence on conservative movements goes beyond the halls of Congress and the media industry. His work has inspired a generation of conservative politicians and media personalities who are eager to challenge the mainstream media and fight back against what they perceive as the dominance of liberal narratives. As a key figure in the Trumpist movement, Nunes' legacy will likely be defined by his role in shaping the trajectory of the modern conservative movement and his efforts to reshape the political discourse in America.

As Devin Nunes looks to the future, his legacy remains a subject of intense debate. His contributions to U.S. politics and the conservative movement have been significant, but they are also deeply polarizing. For some, he will always be remembered as a defender of conservative values and a loyal ally to President Trump—someone who fought for rural communities, worked to protect American sovereignty, and championed the causes of ordinary Americans. For others, his role in the Trump-Russia investigation and his efforts to undermine the legitimacy of the political system will forever color his legacy.

What is clear, however, is that Nunes' impact on U.S. politics and media is undeniable. His transition from politician to media executive has further cemented his place in the ongoing battle for control of the political narrative. Whether one sees him as a hero or a villain, there is no denying that Nunes has played a central role in shaping the political discourse of the past decade. His legacy will continue to evolve, and the influence he has had on conservative movements and public discourse will be felt for years to come.

Conclusion

Devin Nunes is a figure whose career has been defined by a mixture of steadfast loyalty, political ambition, and a deep commitment to the ideals he believes in—values that have left an indelible mark on American politics and media. From his early days in California's Central Valley to his controversial tenure as Chairman of the House Intelligence Committee and his subsequent role as the CEO of Trump Media & Technology Group, Nunes' journey has not only shaped the political landscape but also altered the direction of conservative discourse in the United States.

Whether viewed as a defender of conservative principles or as a polarizing figure who has contributed to the deepening divides in American society, Devin Nunes' legacy is one that will endure for years to come. Nunes' career has been marked by both achievements and controversies, each of which has had a significant impact on the political scene. His rise to prominence began in the halls of the U.S. House of Representatives, where he served from 2003 until his departure in 2022.

Nunes' reputation as a staunch advocate for the agricultural community, combined with his deep understanding of national security and intelligence matters, allowed him to make meaningful contributions to U.S. policy. As a representative of California's 21st and 22nd districts, he became known for his advocacy on behalf of rural America, particularly farmers who felt they were being left behind by Washington's urban-centric policies.

Nunes' most notable political achievement, however, came with his appointment as Chairman of the House Intelligence Committee. In this position, Nunes became a central figure in the investigation into Russian interference in the 2016 U.S. presidential election. His role in the Trump-Russia investigation is perhaps the most controversial aspect of his political career. Nunes' steadfast defense of President Trump and his release of the infamous Nunes memo in 2018—accusing the FBI of misconduct during its investigation—created a firestorm of debate across the nation. To his supporters, he was a defender of transparency, exposing what they believed was bias within the FBI. To his critics, he was an enabler of a politically motivated narrative designed to discredit legitimate investigations and protect the Trump administration.

Despite the backlash from his critics, Nunes' tenure on the House Intelligence Committee was influential. He helped shift the direction of the investigation, undermining the work of those who sought to hold Trump accountable for any potential wrongdoing. This deeply partisan stance earned him praise from conservative circles, where he was seen as a hero for his unwavering support of the president. However, it also earned him the ire of those who felt he was willing to compromise the integrity of the intelligence community and the rule of law for partisan gain.

Following his departure from Congress in 2022, Nunes transitioned into a new role as the CEO of Trump Media & Technology Group, a company that sought to create an alternative media platform in response to what he and many others perceived as the liberal bias of mainstream media outlets. Through Truth Social, Trump Media & Technology Group aimed to give conservatives a space to express their views without fear of censorship. This pivot to media was a natural progression for Nunes, who had spent much of his career shaping public opinion and fighting battles in the media.

His leadership in this new venture places him at the heart of the ongoing cultural war between conservative and liberal media, where he continues to play a prominent role in shaping the narratives that resonate with millions of Americans. In addition to his role in media, Nunes has maintained a presence in the world of political commentary and endorsements. His voice remains influential among conservative circles, where he continues to advocate for policies that reflect his belief in smaller government, tax reform, and a strong national defense. His pivot from the halls of Congress to the world of business and media has ensured that his influence in American politics remains potent, even as he steps away from the political spotlight.

Nunes' legacy is multifaceted and complicated, characterized by both contributions to American governance and divisive moments that have shaped political discourse in the 21st century. As a politician, his most lasting impact lies in his unwavering loyalty to conservative values and his role in advancing the Republican agenda during the Trump years. His advocacy for rural America, his defense of President Trump, and his role in key legislative efforts have solidified his position as a champion of conservative causes. Yet, his legacy is not without controversy.

At the heart of Nunes' legacy is his role in the political transformation of the Republican Party during the Trump era. Nunes embraced Trump's populist agenda with fervor, becoming one of the most vocal defenders of the president and a key figure in advancing his political goals. Nunes' actions in the House Intelligence Committee, his release of the Nunes memo, and his relentless attack on the FBI and the broader intelligence community all played a role in cementing Trump's grip on the Republican Party and galvanizing the conservative base. Nunes became the embodiment of a new breed of Republican politics—one that prioritized loyalty to the president over traditional conservative values and institutional norms.

The most lasting impact of Nunes' political career may be his role in the broader conservative movement. As a figure who was deeply enmeshed in the rise of Trumpism, Nunes played a pivotal role in shaping the narrative that continues to define much of the modern conservative landscape. His embrace of populism, his advocacy for nationalism, and his unyielding defense of Trump have helped set the stage for the future of the Republican Party, ensuring that the GOP remains a party that is shaped by Trump's influence long after his presidency.

However, Nunes' legacy in the political arena is also marked by his involvement in some of the most divisive and polarizing moments of the past decade. His efforts to undermine the Trump-Russia investigation, his release of the Nunes memo, and his fierce loyalty to President Trump all contributed to a deepening of the partisan divide in American politics. While his supporters see him as a courageous defender of conservative values and a voice for those who feel silenced by the political establishment, his critics view him as a figure who prioritized partisan politics over truth, accountability, and national security.

In this way, Nunes' legacy is one that has both solidified his position as a conservative icon and further entrenched the divisions within American politics. In the world of media, Nunes' transition from politics to business has allowed him to shape public discourse in new ways. As CEO of Trump Media & Technology Group, he is at the helm of an effort to challenge the mainstream media's dominance and provide a platform for conservative voices. Through Truth Social and other media ventures, Nunes aims to create an alternative space for conservatives to express their views without fear of censorship.

His work in this area ensures that his legacy will continue to influence the media landscape, particularly within the conservative sphere. Beyond politics and media, Nunes' legacy is one that will be felt in the broader cultural and ideological battles that continue to define America's political landscape. As a figure who has championed conservative causes and fought back against what he perceives as liberal bias in the media, Nunes will continue to be a key figure in the cultural wars that shape the nation. His influence will likely endure as the country grapples with issues of media control, political polarization, and the future of American democracy.

As we close this exploration of Devin Nunes' life and legacy, it's important to recognize the profound impact his career has had on U.S. politics, media, and beyond. Whether you view him as a hero or a villain, his influence on American politics is undeniable, and his legacy will continue to shape the political discourse for years to come. Thank you for taking the time to learn about the complex and multifaceted journey of Devin Nunes, a figure whose career has been defined by both triumph and controversy.

Your interest in understanding his story is appreciated, and we hope this biography has provided valuable insights into the life of a man whose influence will continue to be felt in the world of politics and media for years to come.

www.ingramcontent.com/pod-product-compliance
Lightning Source LLC
Chambersburg PA
CBHW071110240526
45469CB00006BD/2420